DATE DUE

JV 2 00			

DEMCO

Parade Mania

By Ed and Ruth Radlauer

AN ELK GROVE BOOK

CP CHILDRENS PRESS, CHICAGO

STRATEGIES, a teaching guide for using MANIA BOOKS for reading instruction, is available along with a cassette recording and MANIA CARDS (skill-builders) to accompany this book.

For assistance with photography, the authors thank
Ronnie and Bill Lomas of *Pageantry Productions, Inc.*
of Lynwood, California

Photo credits:
    Public Relations, Macy's Department Store, New York City, pages 25 and 30

Library of Congress Cataloging in Publication Data

Radlauer, Ed.
  Parade mania.

  (Mania books)
  "An Elk Grove book."
  Summary: Uses simple vocabulary to discuss
parts of a parade.
    1. Parades — Juvenile literature. ·
[1. Parades] I. Radlauer, Ruth Shaw.
II. Title. III. Series: Radlauer mania book.
GT3980.R33   791'.6   82-4133
ISBN 0-516-07793-7   AACR2

1 2 3 4 5 6 7 8 9 10 11 12 13 14 15 R 88 87 86 85 84 83 82

A RADLAUER
Mania
Book

CREATED FOR CHILDRENS PRESS BY
*RADLAUER PRODUCTIONS INCORPORATED

Parade mania?
Yes, it's parade mania.
Start your parade with flags—

—and more flags.

Start your parade with horses—

—and more horses.

Dress up your cat for a parade.

Dress up your cat for a parade?

You can take your dog
in a parade.

Take your dog
in a parade?

In a parade,
you can go on one wheel.

You can go on one wheel
or two wheels.

13

In a parade,
you can go on one wheel,
two wheels, or three wheels.

Three wheels?

Make a mask—

—and take your mask
in a parade.

You can make a mask from a box.

Make your mask from a box
or a paper sack.
Make a mask from a paper sack?

Your parade needs balloons.

Your parade needs balloons
and feathers, lots of feathers.

Your parade needs pink fans.

A parade needs pink fans
and a pink float.

Your parade float—

—can be a boat.
Can a parade boat float?

A parade needs clowns—

—lots of clowns.

A parade needs music—

—lots of music.

Parade mania?

Yes, it's parade mania.

Parade Words